S N A P S H O T S   I N   H I S T O R Y

THE REPUBLICAN PARTY

The Story of the Grand Old Party

W9-DIG-027

by Dale Anderson

THE REPUBLICAN PARTY

The Story of the Grand Old Party

by Dale Anderson

Content Adviser: Tom Lansford, Ph.D., Assistant Dean and
Associate Professor of Political Science, College of Arts
and Letters, University of Southern Mississippi

Reading Adviser: Katie Van Sluys, Ph.D.,
School of Education, DePaul University

Compass Point Books Minneapolis, Minnesota

THE REPUBLICAN PARTY

⊕ COMPASS POINT BOOKS

3109 West 50th Street, #115
Minneapolis, MN 55410

Visit Compass Point Books on the Internet at
www.compasspointbooks.com
or e-mail your request to
custserv@compasspointbooks.com

For Compass Point Books
Jennifer VanVoorst, Jaime Martens, XNR Productions, Inc.,
Catherine Neitge, Keith Griffin, and Carol Jones

Produced by White-Thomson Publishing Ltd.

For White-Thomson Publishing
Stephen White-Thomson, Susan Crean, Amy Sparks,
Tinstar Design Ltd., Tom Lansford, Peggy Bresnick Kendler,
Will Hare, and Timothy Griffin

The official elephant logo of the RNC and the phrase "Grand Old
Party" were provided courtesy of the Republican National Committee.

Library of Congress Cataloging-in-Publication Data
Anderson, Dale, 1953–
  The Republican Party : the story of the Grand Old Party / by Dale
Anderson.
      p. cm. — (Snapshots in history)
  Includes bibliographical references and index.
  ISBN-13: 978-0-7565-2449-4 (library binding)
  ISBN-10: 0-7565-2449-0 (library binding)
  ISBN-13: 978-0-7565-3171-3 (paperback)
  ISBN-10: 0-7565-3171-3 (paperback)
  1. Republican Party (U.S. : 1854–)—History—Juvenile literature. 2.
United States—Politics and government—Juvenile literature. I. Title.
II. Series.
  JK2356.A63 2007
  324.2734—dc22   2006034098

CONTENTS

A Surprising Election

Chapter

1

On September 3, 1856, members of Wisconsin's Republican Party staged a mass rally in the small town of Beloit, on the state's border with Illinois. As many as 20,000 people crowded into the town, which had a population of around 4,200. Opening the daylong event was a two-hour parade featuring hundreds of marchers and 10 marching bands that blared out patriotic songs.

The parade included a float with 32 young women. Thirty-one of them, dressed in white, represented each of the nation's states. The other was dressed in black, symbolizing mourning. She stood for the territory of Kansas, where fighting was going on between two groups of settlers—those who wanted Kansas to allow slavery and those who did not.

The situation in Kansas played a major role in the speeches at the Beloit rally. Republican speakers blamed the violence there on Southerners, who wanted slavery to spread from their part of the country to Western territories.

News accounts of the fighting in Kansas inflamed the bitterness between Northerners and Southerners during the 1856 election.

The Beloit rally was staged to drum up support for the Republican Party during the campaign leading up to the presidential election of 1856. This election marked the first time that American voters directly addressed the issue of slavery.

Political passions ran high that election year. Many people feared that the fighting in Kansas hinted at worse violence to come. Senator Thomas Hart Benton of Missouri expressed the alarm that many felt: "We are treading upon a volcano that is liable at any moment to burst forth and overwhelm the nation."

The Republican Party was only 2 years old and in 1856 was running its first candidate for president. Party leaders had picked explorer John C. Frémont for two reasons. First, he was well known across the country and was seen by many Americans as a hero. Second, he had no political record, which meant voters could not be upset by any of his past positions or decisions.

JOHN CHARLES FRÉMONT

John Charles Frémont gained national fame in the early 1840s when he led an expedition across the Rocky Mountains to find the best overland route to the Oregon Territory. His wife, Jessie Benton Frémont, helped him write a dramatic account of his explorations that gained him the nickname "Pathfinder." When the Mexican War began in 1846, Frémont was exploring in California, which then belonged to Mexico. When Americans living in California declared their independence from Mexico, Frémont quickly put himself in charge, an action that further increased his popularity.

In an age before television and radio, political parties had to use other means to make their candidates' names known to voters. One method was to provide sheet music for songs about the party and its candidate.

The Republican Party left little doubt where it stood on the crucial issue of slavery, however. The platform of 1856 boldly stated that Republicans opposed any law with "the purpose of establishing slavery in the territories of the United States."

Running against Frémont was Democratic Party candidate James Buchanan of Pennsylvania. Buchanan was an experienced politician who had served in the U.S. House of Representatives and the Senate and had been the nation's secretary of state. He had the advantage of heading the most organized—and the oldest—party in the race. The Democrats were willing to allow slavery in the territories, which made them strong in the slaveholding South.

A third candidate, Millard Fillmore of New York, was also trying to win the White House that year. Like Buchanan, Fillmore had a great deal of political experience. He had been elected vice president in 1848 and had served more than two years as president after President Zachary Taylor died in 1850.

Fillmore ran on the ticket of the Know-Nothing Party, also only a few years old. The Know-Nothings had at first ignored the slavery issue and called for new laws that would slow immigration, give preference to native-born Americans for government jobs, and lengthen the time an immigrant had to wait before becoming an American citizen to 21 years.

This party was called Know-Nothing because it had begun as a society whose members were pledged to secrecy. When asked about the group's meetings, members were supposed to say, "I know nothing." Officially, however, the party was called the American Party.

OUR COUNTRY AND HER FLAG.

NATIVE

AMERICANS.

The Know-Nothings tried to appeal to native-born Americans who were worried about the rising number of immigrants reaching the country.

The 1856 presidential campaign was a spirited one. Republicans held rallies and marched in long parades, chanting their slogan—"Free Soil, Free Labor, Free Men, Frémont"—and carrying banners that showed the candidate's face.

13

THE TWO-PARTY SYSTEM

When the United States was founded, there were no political parties. By the 1790s, though, two had developed: the Federalists and the Democratic-Republicans. By the 1820s, the Federalist Party had disappeared, and the Democratic-Republicans dominated political life. In the early 1830s, the Democratic-Republicans divided into the Democratic Party and the Whig Party.

By 1856, the issue of slavery had destroyed the Whig Party. Most Southern Whigs left their party to join the Democrats, who defended slavery. Some Northern Whigs joined the Know-Nothing Party, but many took part in forming the Republican Party.

Democrats held their own parades, with banners asking Americans to vote for "Buck and Breck," referring to presidential candidate Buchanan and his running mate, John C. Breckinridge. Meanwhile, members of the Know-Nothing Party thundered their slogan, "Americans must rule America."

Editorial writers appealed to voters' emotions. Republican writers warned that Southerners would keep extending slavery until it was established in the North—and then Northern workers would lose their jobs. Democrats said that if Frémont won the election, the Southern states would leave the Union.

Personal attacks on the candidates were part of the campaign, too. Most Americans in 1856 were Protestants, and many of them had negative feelings toward Roman Catholics. These negative feelings reflected hundreds of years of mistrust

THE RIGHT MAN FOR THE RIGHT PLACE.

and occasional fighting between Protestants and Catholics. Aware of this prejudice, both the Know-Nothings and the Democrats spread rumors that Frémont was a Catholic. Though the claims were not true, they cut into Frémont's support.

In November 1856, voters went to the polls in large numbers—in many states, more than 80 percent of eligible voters cast ballots. In the end, Buchanan gained the presidency by winning 174 electoral votes to Frémont's 114. Fillmore could manage to win only one state's electoral votes.

An 1856 pro-American Party cartoon featured Know-Nothing candidate Millard Fillmore (center) holding off Republican John C. Frémont (left) and Democrat James Buchanan.

15

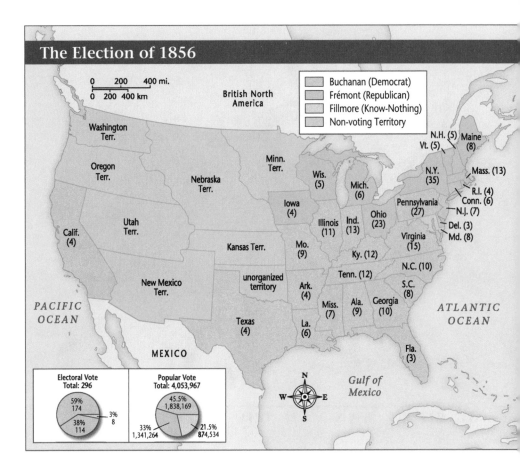

The Election of 1856

0   200   400 mi.
0 200 400 km

British North America

Buchanan (Democrat)
Frémont (Republican)
Fillmore (Know-Nothing)
Non-voting Territory

Washington Terr.

Oregon Terr.

Minn. Terr.

Nebraska Terr.

Wis. (5)

Mich. (6)

N.H. (5) Maine (8)

Vt. (5)

N.Y. (35) Mass. (13)

R.I. (4)

Conn. (6)

Iowa (4)

Pennsylvania (27) N.J. (7)

Utah Terr.

Illinois (11) Ind. (13) Ohio (23)

Del. (3)

Calif. (4)

Kansas Terr.

Mo. (9)

Virginia (15) Md. (8)

Ky. (12)

N.C. (10)

Tenn. (12)

New Mexico Terr.

unorganized territory

Ark. (4)

S.C. (8)

Miss. (7) Ala. (9) Georgia (10)

PACIFIC OCEAN

ATLANTIC OCEAN

Texas (4)

La. (6)

MEXICO

Fla. (3)

Gulf of Mexico

N
W   E
S

Electoral Vote
Total: 296

59%
174

3%
8

38%
114

Popular Vote
Total: 4,053,967

45.5%
1,838,169

33%
1,341,264

21.5%
874,534

All of Frémont's votes in the 1856 election came from states in the Northeast and Great Lakes regions.

Although Frémont lost the 1856 election, his close second was an impressive showing for an inexperienced candidate leading a 2-year-old party. The result left Republicans very happy. They felt that even though they had been defeated, they were victorious. Poet John Greenleaf Whittier, who was a Republican, was optimistic about the party's chances in the next presidential election: "If months have well-nigh [almost] won the field, What may not four years do?"

Republicans also took heart from results in other races that year. They captured 92 seats in the House of Representatives, compared with only 14 for the Know-Nothing Party. While the Democrats would have 128 seats, the Republicans had clearly become the chief opposition party. In addition, Republicans had enough power in state legislatures—which chose senators at that time—to gain 20 seats in the Senate. Again, this was fewer than the Democrats' 37 seats, but it dwarfed the mere five seats that were held by the Know-Nothings.

Electoral Votes

The president and vice president are not elected by voters but by electors. Most states award all their electoral votes to the candidate who wins the popular vote. The candidate with the majority of electoral votes then becomes president. These votes are not automatically registered, however. Special people called electors cast these ballots. Until the early 1800s, the winner of the most electoral votes won the presidency, and the runner-up became vice president. That changed with the 12th Amendment, which called for electors to vote separately for both a president and vice president. Today candidates for president and vice president run as a team and are elected together.

Over the next 150-plus years, the Republican Party would grow and change. From its antislavery origins, it would continue to take moral stands on certain issues. It would also become known as the party of business and of national defense. And the Republican Party would come to dominate American politics for long stretches of time in the following century and a half. ◣

17

The Republicans Win the White House

Chapter

2

For the new Republican Party, the 1856 election was an encouraging defeat. The party had gained a lot of ground in the two years since it was first organized.

The Republican Party had formed in 1854 in opposition to the Kansas-Nebraska Act, a law that allowed slavery in Kansas or Nebraska if the majority of residents wanted it. Many Northern Whigs felt this law created opportunities for slavery to expand, and they began meeting in several Northern states to form a new political party to fight it.

Exactly where the party formed is debated. The people of Exeter, New Hampshire, say that several people met in a hotel there on October 12, 1853, to discuss forming a new party. Republicans in Crawfordsville, Iowa, say that the first party meeting took place in their town in February 1854. Unfortunately, the papers documenting that meeting were destroyed in a fire. Michigan Republicans point to a statewide convention held in the city of Jackson on July 6, 1854. They say that this meeting should be considered the origin of the party because it was the first group to use the name Republican, to adopt a party platform, and to nominate candidates for office. Most historians, however, agree that a meeting in Ripon, Wisconsin, on March 20, 1854, marks the founding of the Republican Party.

Two years after its formation, the 1856 election gave the new Republican Party national prominence, but the next critical event in the party's growth

The Republican candidates for the 1856 election may not have won, but they established the new party as a strong political force.

came in 1857. On March 6, the U.S. Supreme Court ruled in the case of *Dred Scott v. Sandford*. Dred Scott, an enslaved African-American, had sued for his freedom on the ground that he had lived for some time in a free state—one where slavery did not exist. The court denied him his freedom, but it also went much further. It ruled that African-Americans, either free or enslaved, could not be citizens of the United States. The court also said that Congress did not have the power to limit slavery in the territories.

Southern politicians and newspapers declared the wisdom of the court's ruling. Newspaper editors in the free states complained bitterly that the court had misread the U.S. Constitution. Editor William Cullen Bryant denounced the ruling in the *New York Evening Post*:

What's in a Name?

Newspaper editor Horace Greeley, an important figure in the early Republican Party, was influential in naming the new party. He promoted the name Republican for two reasons. First, it linked the new party to the Democratic-Republican Party, which had been founded in the 1790s by Thomas Jefferson. Second, the name was connected to complaints that the national government was dominated by the "Slave Power," the Southern plantation owners who were working to control the federal government and spread slavery nationwide. By referring to themselves as Republicans, members of the new party were aligning themselves with the American values of civic virtue and democracy instead of corruption and aristocracy.

Are we to accept, without question ... that hereafter it shall be a slaveholders' instead of the freemen's Constitution? Never! Never!

Republican Abraham Lincoln of Illinois echoed these ideas in 1858, when he ran against Democrat Stephen Douglas for a seat in the U.S. Senate. In a series of debates, Lincoln and Douglas sparred over the issue of slavery in the territories.

Abraham Lincoln made a name for himself as an antislavery candidate during his campaign for the Senate.

21

In speech after speech, Lincoln identified himself with the basic Republican position:

> *We think it [slavery] is a moral, a social, and a political wrong. ... We also oppose it as an evil so far as it seeks to spread itself. We insist on the policy that shall restrict it to its present limits.*

Douglas won the Senate election, but the debates made Lincoln famous across the country. As a result, Lincoln became one of the leading candidates for the Republican nomination for president in 1860.

Though Lincoln had lost the 1858 election for senator, Republicans made many gains. They picked up 19 seats in the House of Representatives from the free states. In fact, several Republican candidates won seats in states that Frémont had lost in 1856, showing that the party was on the rise. The strength of the Know-Nothing Party, meanwhile, had dwindled to only a few seats. Though just a few years old, the Republican Party stood poised to become the main challenger to the Democratic Party.

Though blocking the spread of slavery was the most important issue for Republicans, they pushed other issues as well. They wanted to begin building a transcontinental railroad that would link states east of the Mississippi River with California on the Pacific Ocean. They hoped to set up state colleges to teach good farming techniques. They wanted a

DIVISIONS IN THE KNOW-NOTHING PARTY

The Know-Nothing Party, like the Whigs, collapsed because of differences over slavery. When the party formed in 1854, Southern members wanted to ignore the slavery issue. Many Northern members agreed, but a vocal minority insisted on a strong statement against the Kansas-Nebraska Act. The debate was renewed in 1856, when the Know-Nothings chose Millard Fillmore as their candidate for president. When the 1856 convention approved a statement on slavery that Northern members thought to be too mild, more than 70 of them walked out of the convention. This conflict seriously weakened the party, and by 1859, the party had broken apart.

homesteading law that would give people land in the territories at little cost. And they wanted Congress to pass tariffs to protect American industries. Since many of these ideas were old Whig issues and many Republicans had been Whigs before, it was easy for the new party to adopt them.

Republican newspaper editor Horace Greeley thought that the Republican Party's platform would help it win votes, as he explained in a letter to a friend:

> *I know the country is not anti-slavery. It will only swallow a little anti–slavery in a great deal of sweetening. An antislavery man ... cannot be elected; but a tariff, ... Pacific railroad, free-homestead man may succeed although he is anti-slavery.*

As the nation neared the 1860 election, it was on the verge of breaking apart. Many Southerners feared that the Republicans, once in power, would not only try to stop the spread of slavery, but would move to outlaw it altogether. They declared that if a Republican won the presidency, the South would leave the Union.

The main obstacle to a Republican victory would be a united Democratic Party—but unity was something that eluded the Democrats. Hostility and anger marred the Democratic National Convention in Charleston, South Carolina, in April 1860. Members from the free states and slave states clashed over their party's platform and nominee. At one point, the more numerous free-state delegates pushed through a platform statement on slavery that Southerners did not like. Fifty angry delegates from the South left the convention hall. Remaining members of the convention voted to adjourn the meeting for six weeks and try again.

JOHN BROWN'S RAID

In 1859, abolitionist John Brown led a small force of armed men to seize guns and ammunition in an armory in Harpers Ferry, Virginia. Brown's goal had been to use the weapons to start a revolt of slaves— precisely what Southerners feared the most. After Brown and his followers were seized by U.S. troops, the state of Virginia quickly tried him. The jury found him guilty, and he was hanged. Most Southerners saw Brown as the worst sort of criminal. Democrats quickly tried to lay the blame for Brown's raid on Republicans and claimed that a slave revolt was the logical outcome of Republican speeches attacking slavery.

The same bitterness destroyed the second convention, held in Baltimore, Maryland. This time an even larger number of delegates left. Those who remained finally nominated Stephen Douglas, the U.S. senator from Illinois, but his chances of winning the election were small.

After leaving the Democratic convention in Charleston, Southern delegates got together to discuss their next move.

Soon after, the Southern delegates who had left called a new convention and named then-Vice President John C. Breckinridge of Kentucky as their candidate. The Democratic Party had split in two.

Meanwhile, several leading Republicans vied for the nomination of their young party. The victor was Abraham Lincoln, who held no political office at the time. Lincoln was chosen partly because the convention was held in his home state of Illinois, partly because he had shrewd campaign managers, and partly because he had impressed other Republicans with his speeches. Swallowing their disappointment, the other candidates quickly rallied behind Lincoln. The division among the Democrats made the possibility of winning the election so strong that Republicans did not want to jeopardize their chances with disunity of their own.

A fourth candidate for president also emerged. A new group called the Constitutional Union Party picked John Bell of Tennessee as its candidate. This very small group was composed of a few former Whigs and members of the old Know-Nothing Party who did not want the country to break apart over the slavery issue.

When the election took place that fall, Lincoln could not win a majority of the popular vote, but he gained a clear electoral majority of 180 votes out of a total of 303. Significantly, he won 60 percent of the popular votes in the free states.

In addition to Lincoln's presidential victory, Republicans had other successes in the 1860 election. They won the governorships of every free state and 108 seats in the House of Representatives. When the state legislatures filled the open Senate seats, the Republicans had 31 senators. ◣

After taking the oath of office in 1861, Lincoln tried to offer calming words to Southerners, but they largely fell on deaf ears.

The Party of Freedom

Early in 1861, Republicans took control of the White House and Congress for the first time, but they led a fractured country. Starting in late 1860, seven Southern states acted on their earlier threat and seceded, or withdrew, from the Union. These states were South Carolina, Georgia, Florida, Alabama, Mississippi, Louisiana, and Texas. After seceding from the Union, they formed the Confederate States of America, or the Confederacy. Several other slave states teetered on the edge of secession as well.

President Lincoln thought secession was illegal. Still, he did not wish to use force against the Confederacy. He worried that doing so would only help to convince the slave states that still remained to leave the Union as well.

On April 16, 1861, Confederate forces in Charleston, South Carolina, settled the question of whether to use force by firing on Fort Sumter, a Union-held fortress in Charleston harbor. The Civil War had begun.

Lincoln quickly asked the governors of all states in the Union to call up militia troops to end the rebellion. Tens of thousands of men across the North volunteered to join the fight. But as Lincoln had feared, the call for troops led Virginia, North Carolina, Tennessee, and Arkansas to join the Confederacy.

Confederates kept up a steady barrage on Fort Sumter for about a day and a half until the Union soldiers inside surrendered.

When the Civil War began, Lincoln's goal was simply to restore the Union. Many Republicans pushed him to declare an end to slavery, but he did not believe the president had the authority to do that. He also worried that such a step would push four border states out of the Union as well. These states—Delaware, Maryland, Kentucky, and Missouri—all allowed slavery but had remained loyal to the Union.

Northerners blamed the Civil War on Southern leaders, shown in a cartoon as the heads of a mythical monster being attacked by a Union general.

THE HERCULES OF THE UNION,
SLAYING THE GREAT DRAGON OF SECESSION.

During the summer of 1862, though, Lincoln's view of the situation changed. He now felt that the border states were firmly in the Union. He also came to believe that the Union Army would accept granting slaves their freedom.

Lincoln took decisive action. In September 1862, he announced that on January 1, 1863, if the Confederate states refused to rejoin the Union, he would free the slaves in parts of those states still under Confederate control. Slaves in the border states and in parts of the South controlled by the Union Army would not be freed, since Lincoln did not believe he had the authority to free the slaves in these areas.

OTHER REPUBLICAN BUSINESS

The Civil War dominated the attention of the government from 1861 to 1865. Still, the Republicans who controlled the government took steps as well. Three laws passed in 1862 put in place key Republican goals—and shaped the future of the country. The Homestead Act gave parcels of land in the Western territories to people willing to farm that land for five years. After the Civil War, thousands of Americans took advantage of this law. The Pacific Railroad Act gave land grants to two railroad companies so they could build a railroad from Missouri to the Pacific Coast. The companies completed that work in 1869, linking the country by rail. Finally, the Morrill Land Grant Act gave federal land to each state, which could sell the land to raise money to build state colleges. The schools that resulted form a core part of American public colleges and universities.

The North now had two goals in fighting the Civil War: restoring the Union, and freeing the slaves. The Republican Party was on the side of the North in support of unity and freedom.

Changing the goals of the war did not necessarily bring victory any closer for the Union, however. The fighting dragged on for many months. Lincoln sensed growing gloom in the Union during the summer of 1864, as a new presidential election neared. That fall, voters would either endorse Lincoln's handling of the war and re-elect him or show their disapproval by electing his opponent.

Democratic candidate George B. McClellan ran against Lincoln in the 1864 election. McClellan had once commanded the chief Union forces and enjoyed great popularity among his troops. The Democrats hoped to win the votes of Union soldiers, who they believed were tired of the fighting. The Democratic platform hinted that the party would reverse Lincoln's Emancipation Proclamation and boldly declared that it wanted an end to the war:

> *This convention does explicitly declare ... that after four years of failure to restore the Union by the experiment of war, ... justice, humanity, liberty, and the public welfare demand that immediate efforts be made for a cessation of hostilities ... to the end that ... peace may be restored on the basis of the Federal Union of the States.*

Lincoln became convinced that he would lose the election. In September 1864, though, Union armies gained a breakthrough. General William T. Sherman led his army deep into the Confederacy

and captured Atlanta, Georgia. Sherman's news buoyed Northern spirits once again—and helped produce overwhelming Republican victories in the fall. Lincoln won re-election, and Republicans gained large majorities in both houses of Congress. Republicans also held the governorship and state legislature in all but three states in the Union—Kentucky, Delaware, and New Jersey.

Fighting in the Civil War continued throughout Lincoln's campaign in the 1864 presidential election.

33

General William T. Sherman's capture of Atlanta ended many months during which the Union Army showed little progress but suffered many casualties.

The election gave Lincoln and the Republicans a mandate to carry on the Civil War—and to formally end slavery. On January 31, 1865, Republicans in Congress—joined by a few Democrats—passed an amendment to the U.S. Constitution to abolish slavery across the country. By the year's end, enough states had ratified the change to make the 13th Amendment official.

By then, the Civil War had ended. On April 9, 1865, Confederate General Robert E. Lee surrendered the tattered remains of his army to Union General Ulysses S. Grant. Over the next weeks and months, other Southern armies soon followed, and the fighting ceased.

The end of the war launched the period called Reconstruction, when the Southern states formed new governments and rejoined the Union. Lincoln favored a generous policy that would allow the Southern states back into the Union if just a small percentage of voters swore loyalty to the United States. Republican leaders in Congress, however, wanted stricter rules, including some guarantees that the freed slaves would enjoy equal rights.

In time, Lincoln and the congressional leaders might have worked out their differences, but we will never know. On April 14, 1865, Lincoln was assassinated by John Wilkes Booth, an actor who sympathized with the South. The murdered president became a hero to Republicans, even though many of them had criticized him during his term in office. For many decades to follow, the Republican Party referred to itself as the Party of Lincoln.

Vice President Andrew Johnson—a Democrat— stepped into the presidency, but he soon clashed with Republicans in Congress. Over the next three years, Johnson tried to put in place policies that would easily bring Southern states back into the Union and allow former Confederates to govern again. But Republicans in Congress passed bills that were tough on white Southerners and took steps to try to ensure equal rights for African-Americans. Johnson did not think African-Americans should have equal rights and vetoed several of the laws, but Republicans in Congress overrode the vetoes.

The Freedmen's Bureau built schools in the South so newly freed African–Americans could gain skills they had previously been denied.

These Republican-backed laws remade the South. Congress created an agency to help former slaves make the transition to freedom. This agency, called the Freedmen's Bureau, set up schools for the freed slaves and helped them find paying work. Republicans in Congress sent troops to the South to ensure the safety of African-Americans. They also tried to protect the rights of African-Americans

with the 14th Amendment, which stated clearly that they were citizens and guaranteed them equal rights. By 1870, all the former Confederate states had formed new governments, approved the 14th Amendment, and rejoined the Union.

By this time, a new president sat in the White House. In 1868, Republicans had nominated war hero Ulysses S. Grant, who easily won the election, even taking six states of the former Confederacy—North Carolina, South Carolina, Florida, Tennessee, Alabama, and Arkansas.

Those victories signaled a change in the political geography of the country. From its start, the Republican Party had been a party of the free states—those in the Northeast, along the Great Lakes, and on the West Coast. Now it had strength in the South as well, largely from African-Americans grateful to the Republicans for ending slavery.

Still, trouble lurked in that part of the country. Some white Southerners opposed to the changes formed groups like the Ku Klux Klan, which used violence and threats to try to intimidate African-Americans. Congress responded by passing the 15th Amendment, an antidiscrimination amendment aimed at guaranteeing the voting rights of all African-Americans. It also passed laws allowing the government to punish members of the Klan and other groups that targeted African-Americans. Eventually, the wave of violence against African-Americans subsided.

By the time the 1876 election approached, Grant had served two terms. The Republicans nominated Governor Rutherford B. Hayes of Ohio to follow him. The Democrats chose Governor Samuel Tilden of New York as their candidate. The election was one of the closest in history, but in the end, Hayes seemed to win the electoral vote by one vote, though Tilden had more popular votes. To complicate matters, Democrats challenged the electoral votes in three Southern states.

Congress named a commission of 15 members to settle the dispute. The commission, composed of five members from the Senate, five from the House, and five from the Supreme Court, voted strictly along party lines to give Hayes the victory.

President Rutherford B. Hayes had been an officer in the Union army during the Civil War.

At the same time, Republican leaders told Southern Democrats that if they accepted Hayes' election, the president would withdraw remaining federal troops from the South. The Democrats agreed, and on March 5, 1877, Hayes took the oath of office. Within two months, the last federal troops had left the South. Reconstruction was over.

Abandoned by the Republicans, African-Americans in the South suffered badly. White-dominated Southern governments began passing segregation laws that put whites and blacks in separate schools, parks, trains, and other public places. The facilities provided to African-Americans were always inferior to those provided to whites. Other new laws blocked African-Americans from voting. Though these laws violated the 15th Amendment, the federal government—dominated by Republicans—did nothing.

THE REPUBLICAN ELEPHANT

The idea of an elephant as the unofficial symbol of the Republican Party was originated by political cartoonist Thomas Nast in a drawing published in 1874. At first, Nast used the animal to stand for the Republican vote, but it quickly became adapted to represent the party itself. He also popularized the donkey as a symbol of the Democratic Party. The two parties have differing views on the meanings of their respective animals. A Democratic publication stated it as such: "The Democrats think of the elephant as bungling, stupid, pompous and conservative— but the Republicans think it is dignified, strong and intelligent. On the other hand, the Republicans regard the donkey as stubborn, silly and ridiculous—but the Democrats claim it is humble, homely, smart, courageous and loveable."

The Party Grows and Changes

Chapter

4

After Reconstruction, Republican strength in the South disappeared. The Democratic Party, led by whites bent on segregation, controlled that region for the next 90 years. In the 21 states from the Northeast to the Great Plains, however, Republicans dominated.

Several factors led to this dominance. The Republicans remained identified as the party that had won the Civil War. Oliver Morton, a Republican who served at different times as governor of Indiana and as a senator from that state, put the situation bluntly: "While it may be true that not every Democrat is a traitor, every traitor is a Democrat."

Republicans were also the party of Protestants, who outnumbered Roman Catholics in the country. As many as 80 percent of the members of some Protestant denominations had voted Republican. Ministers urged their followers to do so because the party took several positions these ministers favored. For instance, Republicans supported laws that closed businesses on Sundays, and many Republicans backed temperance laws. Republicans also worked to pass laws that blocked giving government aid to Catholic-run schools.

Similarly, Republicans stood as the party of native-born Americans. The nativism that had fueled the Know-Nothing Party had not died out in the 1850s, and many native-born Americans disliked the Democratic Party because it appealed to immigrants.

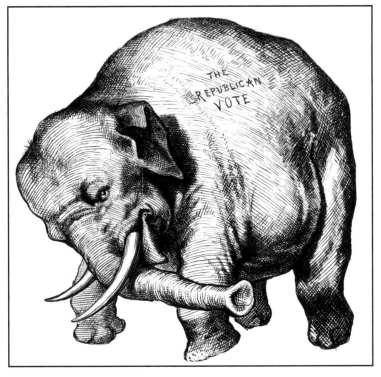

An 1874 Thomas Nast cartoon marks the first appearance of the elephant as a symbol of the Republican Party.

Republicans also worked to pass laws favoring business. Some of these laws helped big corporations, while others were meant to promote opportunities for ordinary people to get ahead. Republicans thought helping business and promoting wealth would help the country build a strong economy—and lead other Americans to success. As Abraham Lincoln had said in 1863:

> *That some should be rich shows that others may become rich, and hence is just encouragement to industry and enterprise.*

Finally, Republicans succeeded because they controlled patronage. The party in power decided who got government jobs. Once in a job, workers were expected to contribute some of their earnings back to the party or risk being fired. The political bosses who led the party used that money to fund campaign efforts like printing pamphlets and banners, holding rallies, and providing favors to voters. Some bosses also took some of the money for themselves. This practice was not unique to Republicans; Democrats did the same thing.

The American public began to turn against the patronage system in the 1870s, when corruption in Congress and the Grant administration led critics to call for a new system for staffing government. They wanted a civil-service system, in which people gained government jobs only after they passed an exam. The issue came to a head in 1881. On July 2 of that year, Republican President

James A. Garfield was shot by Charles Guiteau, who was upset over having been denied a government job. Garfield eventually died from his wounds.

Garfield's assassination led to a public outcry for civil-service reform. Vice President Chester Arthur took up the cause, and, with his support, Congress passed the Pendleton Act in 1883. Under the new

Shot in the back, President James Garfield lingered painfully for more than two months before he died.

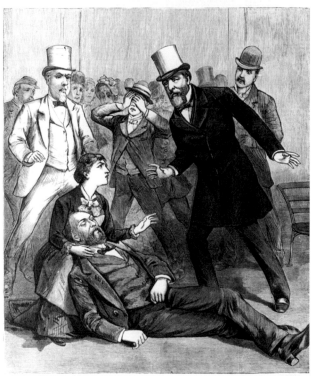

WASHINGTON, D. C.— THE ATTACK ON THE PRESIDENT'S LIFE— MRS. SMITH SUPPORTING THE PRESIDENT WHILE AWAITING THE ARRIVAL OF THE AMBULANCE.—FROM SKETCHES BY OUR SPECIAL ARTIST A DEEGRATE, AND C. UPHAM.—SEE PAGE 335.

law, a large share of jobs in the federal government could only be obtained by taking and passing a civil- service exam.

The Pendleton Act ushered in a new age in the federal government—but it did not end party patronage. The parties simply shifted their attention to the states, where state bosses built up large and powerful organizations.

It was around this time that the Republican Party came to be known as the Grand Old Party, or the GOP. The nickname first appeared in the *Boston Herald* in 1884 and was later picked up by other newspapers. The name is somewhat curious, since the Democratic Party is actually more than 30 years older.

In 1884 and again in 1892, the Democrats took hold of the White House when Grover Cleveland won the presidential elections. Benjamin Harrison, a Republican, served one term in between. Four years after Cleveland's second victory, the Republicans were back with a well-organized, well-funded campaign on behalf of William McKinley. McKinley's presidential victory launched the Republicans on another period in which they dominated national politics. Between 1897 and 1933, six Republicans held the White House for all but eight years. The Republicans also controlled the House for 28 of those 36 years, and the Senate for 30 of the 36.

William McKinley was the fifth Republican president of the late 1800s born in Ohio, a stronghold of the party. Grant, Hayes, Garfield, and Harrison were the others.

In the early part of this period, Republicans began to promote an aggressive foreign policy. Business leaders and Republicans in Congress began to call for the United States to follow the example of European countries and take foreign lands as colonies.

One target was the Hawaiian Islands. In 1893, American plantation owners had overthrown the ruling queen and declared an independent republic. Five years later, after much consideration, President McKinley agreed to annex the islands.

At the same time, McKinley was also engaged in the Spanish-American War. Powerful newspaper owners and many Republicans pushed the United States toward a declaration of war against Spain in early 1898.

45

By the end of the year, after stunning victories by American naval and land forces, Spain agreed to a peace treaty. Spain gave up its claims to Cuba and turned over Puerto Rico, Guam, and the Philippines to the United States.

The people of the Philippines wanted independence, but President McKinley would not allow it. He promised them they would eventually have self-rule, but he believed that the United States had to control the islands to prepare them for that condition. He told a group of ministers in 1898:

> *We could not leave them to themselves—they were unfit for self-government. ... [T]here was nothing left for us to do but to take them all [the entire Philippines], and to educate the Filipinos, and uplift and civilize and Christianize them, and by God's grace to do the best we could by them.*

Filipino freedom fighters, however, wanted independence immediately, and they engaged American soldiers in a war that lasted several years.

The United States also exerted influence in Cuba, keeping that island's people from developing their own government until 1903. Even then, the United States insisted on having the right to send troops to Cuba to maintain order any time it thought it necessary.

After McKinley was assassinated in 1901, Vice President Theodore Roosevelt became president and further expanded American power. In 1903, he sent American gunboats to the waters near Panama, which was then a part of Colombia. The boats protected Panamanians as they declared and eventually won independence from Colombia. A representative of Panama's new government then quickly signed a treaty giving the United States the right to build a canal across Panama and to control that canal for 100 years. Though the effort required years of work, the canal was opened in 1914.

Roosevelt also pushed the Republican Party to back important reforms. The growth of businesses in the late 1800s had led to several serious problems. For instance, some corporations joined to form trusts, business arrangements that allowed them to stifle competition. By driving other companies out of an industry, they could set prices and ensure high profits.

Theodore Roosevelt (center, wearing glasses) gained fame leading a volunteer cavalry unit known as the Rough Riders during the Spanish-American War.

Some companies also carried on other unfair or unsafe practices, such as creating advertising that misled consumers or using unsanitary and unhealthful processes to prepare packaged meat. Roosevelt took aim at these abuses of corporate power.

Back in 1890, Congress had passed the Sherman Antitrust Act, giving the government the power to break up trusts. That power was not used until 1902, when Roosevelt moved to break up Northen Securities, a railroad trust. This action and similar steps against other trusts earned Roosevelt the reputation of being a "trust buster."

Roosevelt also backed a law that gave the government power to regulate the rates that railroads charged their customers. He supported the Pure Food and Drug Act and the Meat Inspection Act, both of which tried to ensure the safety of packaged

THEODORE ROOSEVELT

Known as a brilliant, talented, and energetic man, Theodore Roosevelt (1858–1919) was an author, naturalist, hunter, adventurer, and politician. He rose to fame reforming the civil service and the New York City police department. During the Spanish-American War, Roosevelt became a war hero by leading a successful cavalry unit known as the Rough Riders. That status helped him win election as governor of New York in 1898. Once in office, he quickly moved to launch reforms, annoying the Republican political bosses in the state. Hoping to get him out of the way, they persuaded William McKinley to choose Roosevelt as his running mate in his 1900 re-election campaign. McKinley, however, was assassinated shortly after taking office, making Roosevelt president— much to the disappointment of the bosses.

Teddy Roosevelt's presidency in the early 1900s was marked by many reforms.

foods, medicines, and meats. Finally, he protected millions of acres of land in national parks and forest preserves.

Roosevelt was followed as president by William Howard Taft, who had served as Roosevelt's secretary of war. Taft began his term by continuing some of Roosevelt's policies. By 1912, though, Roosevelt believed that Taft had grown too conservative, and he challenged Taft for the Republican nomination for president that year. When the party rejected him and chose Taft, Roosevelt formed a new party—the Progressive Party. That fall, he gained enough support to cost Taft the election. As a result, Democrat Woodrow Wilson was elected to the White House. ◣

49

Successes and Failures

Chapter

5

During the Taft presidency, the Republican Party had grown more conservative and had begun to distance itself from reform. Around 1920, the party changed in its foreign policy, too. In 1917, most Republicans in Congress had voted in favor of the declaration of war against Germany that brought the United States into World War I. But after the war ended, many Republicans wanted to isolate the United States from involvement with foreign affairs. That movement began with a fight against Democratic President Woodrow Wilson's plan of having the United States join a new international organization, the League of Nations.

Wilson hoped that the league would become an instrument for preventing war, but Republicans saw something else. The plans for the league

called for it to settle disputes between countries. Many Republicans saw in this idea the loss of United-States sovereignty, or authority over its own policies. Led by Senator Henry Cabot Lodge of Massachusetts, Republicans in the Senate defeated the treaty setting up the League of Nations.

Republicans wanted little to do with the outside world after World War I ended.

This stance was part of a Republican shift toward isolationism, or the policy of keeping the United States distanced from world affairs. Other trends contributed to this position. During World War I, revolutionaries seized power in Russia and established the world's first Communist state. Many Americans feared that radicals would try something similar in the United States. As a result, the country experienced a Red Scare, a wave of fear over a Communist takeover.

This fear led to widespread mistrust of immigrants, many of whom were thought to have radical political views. In 1921 and again in 1924, Congress passed laws that put sharp limits on immigration. The 1924 Republican Party platform enthusiastically endorsed these changes. Without such limits, it said, the American people "were threatened with mass immigration that would have seriously disturbed our economic life."

Republican positions in the 1920s showed how the party had changed over the years. The Republicans had begun as an antislavery party and had supported equal rights for African–Americans from the time of the Civil War until the middle 1870s. By the 1920s, however, few Republicans had any interest in pushing for an end to the laws that denied African–Americans their rights.

At its birth, the party had opposed the nativism of the Know-Nothing Party. But the party's members were mainly white Protestants, many of whom lived in rural areas. These people had a mistrust of Roman Catholics and immigrants that became more pronounced in the 1920s.

From the start, the party had promoted the growth of business and economic opportunity. To many Republicans, this meant supporting laws like the Homestead Act of 1863 that gave opportunities to ordinary Americans. In the years after the Civil War, though, Republicans came more and more to favor the large corporations that were growing larger and more powerful as the United States developed an industrial economy. In the early 1900s, Theodore Roosevelt had moved to check corporate power, but over the years, Republicans had grown more conservative, and by the 1920s, most Republicans took the more favorable attitude toward big business held by Roosevelt's successor, William Howard Taft.

The nation as a whole was growing more conservative, too. After decades of reform—and after fighting in World War I—Americans wanted calm. That feeling helped propel Republican Warren G. Harding into the White House in 1921. Harding reassured people when he promised what he called a return to normalcy.

Republicans Harding, Calvin Coolidge, and Herbert Hoover were presidents from 1921 to 1933, and they had no interest in further reforms. All

Vice President Calvin Coolidge became president when Warren G. Harding died in office.

53

three favored policies that promoted business. As Coolidge put it, "The chief business of the American people is business." Pro-business policies included low taxes and high tariffs that increased the cost of imported goods and thus helped boost sales of American-made goods.

The pro-business policies of the Republicans worked for a while, and the economy boomed for much of the 1920s. In 1929, though, the country plunged into a deep, lingering economic collapse— the Great Depression. Republican President Hoover was dismayed over the sufferings of Americans who had lost their jobs and their homes or farms. But for a long time, he held to his belief that the federal government did not have the responsibility to help them. He also did not think the government should borrow money, and therefore increase its debt, in order to fund jobs programs.

Hoover did try to take some steps to solve the economic crisis. He backed the creation of the Reconstruction Finance Corporation, which could make loans to businesses in the hopes of stimulating the economy. Still, Hoover did not do enough to get the economy moving again. By the time he faced re-election in 1932, 12 million Americans—nearly a quarter of the work force—were out of work. Many Americans came to blame him for their continued misery, and few Republicans believed he had a chance to win re-election. While they nominated Hoover again, the Republican National Convention was a lifeless affair with no parades and no bands.

Herbert Hoover was highly respected when he became president, in part because he had skillfully organized efforts to provide relief to Europeans after the end of World War I.

As expected, Hoover lost badly in the 1932 election. His Democratic opponent, Franklin D. Roosevelt, won 472 electoral votes to Hoover's 59. The popular vote also went overwhelmingly against Hoover, as nearly two-thirds of all voters preferred Roosevelt.

55

The Great Depression put millions of Americans out of work and caused hardships for many.

During the 1930s, Republicans tried to put the brakes on Roosevelt's New Deal, the name given to programs he developed to revive the American economy. Republicans wanted a smaller, less active federal government and thought that Roosevelt's programs interfered with businesses.

Republicans also fumed in 1940 when Roosevelt ran for an unprecedented third term as president. The Republicans picked a political newcomer, lawyer and businessman Wendell Willkie, as their candidate. Willkie carried on a tireless campaign, logging more than 30,000 miles (48,000 kilometers) of travel, in which he charged that Roosevelt would lead the country into another war. Nevertheless, the president easily won re-election.

When Japanese forces attacked the U.S. naval base at Pearl Harbor, Hawaii, on December 7, 1941, the United States entered World War II, and Republicans rallied with the rest of the country behind the war effort. But they were humiliated in 1944 when Roosevelt won the presidency yet again.

Roosevelt served three full terms and part of a fourth. When Roosevelt died in office in 1947, his vice president, Harry S. Truman, became president. Truman won election in his own right in 1948. Democrats held majorities in the House and Senate for all but two of the Roosevelt-Truman years. The Republican Party had been eclipsed.

MR. REPUBLICAN

One of the most influential Republicans from the 1930s to the early 1950s was Robert Taft (1889–1953), who was known as "Mr. Republican." Son of former President William Howard Taft, the younger Taft reached the U.S. Senate in 1938 and remained there for the rest of his life. In the 1930s, Taft led Republicans in opposing Roosevelt's New Deal and in trying to keep the United States isolated from world problems. Once the Japanese attacked the United States and the country entered World War II, however, Taft supported the war effort. After the war, he strongly opposed American entry into the United Nations. By this time, Republicans who wanted a more aggressive foreign policy outnumbered those like Taft who preferred American isolation. For that reason, Taft never won the prize he sought—his party's presidential nomination.

After World War II ended in 1945, the Soviet Union set up Communist states in several countries in Eastern Europe. A civil war in China ended with Communists taking control of that country, and the northern halves of Korea and Vietnam adopted communism as well. These years marked the beginning of the Cold War—a struggle between the United States and the Soviet Union for influence around the world. Democratic

The powerful Soviet army paraded through Moscow past the tomb of Vladimir Lenin, the founder of the Soviet state. For nearly 50 years, the Soviet Union and United States were locked in the struggle for worldwide influence called the Cold War.

President Truman adopted a policy aimed at preventing the spread of communism by using economic and military aid to other countries. Many Republicans in Congress backed that policy, though they often complained that Truman did not do enough.

In the late 1940s, a second Red Scare swept across the United States. Revelations that some scientists and government officials had given important secret information to the Soviet Union fueled this renewed fear. In 1950, Republican Senator Joseph McCarthy of Wisconsin gained great strength by charging that the government was riddled with Communist spies. McCarthy never proved his charges, however, and his accusations ruined the lives of many people. That year, seven other Republican senators issued what they called a Declaration of Conscience condemning McCarthy's actions. Margaret Chase Smith of Maine wrote the declaration, and explained in a Senate speech:

> *I think it is high time that we [senators] remembered that we have sworn to uphold and defend the Constitution. I think it is high time that we remembered that the Constitution ... speaks not only of the freedom of speech but also of trial by jury instead of trial by accusation.*

Not until 1954, however, did the full Senate formally vote to disapprove of McCarthy's tactics. After that vote, his influence faded.

In 1952, Republicans turned to Dwight Eisenhower, who had led the Allied armies to victory in Europe during World War II, as their nominee for president. Eisenhower won an easy election victory, and after 30 years of Democratic presidents, a Republican president was now in office. He was elected to a second term in 1956.

Eisenhower worked effectively with the Democrat-led Congress to carry out his goals of building a strong national defense and helping the economy continue growing. Eisenhower proposed, and Congress approved, the building of a national highway system. Today the interstate highways

Dwight Eisenhower— nicknamed "Ike"—was a highly popular president who pursued moderate policies.

form the backbone of the country's transportation network. Late in his presidency, Eisenhower also supported steps to improve science and math education in American schools.

Eisenhower was popular with the American people, but that popularity did not extend to his vice president, Richard Nixon. Nixon ran for president against Democratic Senator John F. Kennedy in 1960. In one of the closest elections in history, Nixon lost.

By this time, a rift had developed between conservative and moderate Republicans. While both groups agreed on the need to carry on the Cold War, they differed on several other issues. Moderates were willing to accept more of the changes in the size and scope of the federal government that had been initiated under the New Deal. Conservatives continued to insist that the government should be smaller and play a lesser role in the economy.

In 1964, the conservatives dominated the party and nominated Senator Barry Goldwater of Arizona for president. Goldwater suffered an overwhelming defeat at the hands of Democratic President Lyndon Johnson, but the election signaled the beginning of a shift in American voting patterns. Goldwater won five Southern states, becoming the first Republican to do so since the end of Reconstruction. He won these states because many white voters in the South objected to Johnson's support of laws to end racial segregation.

Republicans began to eye the South as a region where they could make gains. Four years later, in 1968, Republicans regained the White House when Richard Nixon won the presidency. Like Eisenhower, he came from the moderate wing of the party. But Nixon also tried to appeal to conservative voters, especially targeting those in the South. His efforts paid off in his 1972 re-election bid, when he won the electoral votes of all the Southern states.

Richard Nixon was a master of foreign policy and a skilled politician, but he left office in disgrace.

Nixon did not finish his second term, however. During the 1972 campaign, people hired by Nixon advisers broke into the headquarters of the Democratic Party to try to obtain information about its plans for the election. Nixon joined with many of his aides in taking steps to cover up the connection between the burglary and his advisers. It took federal investigators and members of Congress nearly two years to learn the extent of Nixon's involvement. Once it became known, the House of Representatives moved to impeach him. Certain that he would be convicted by the Senate and removed from office, Nixon resigned the presidency.

Vice President Gerald Ford took office as president and, the next month, pardoned Nixon of any crimes he may have committed as president. That decision, and growing economic problems across the country, cost Ford election as president in 1976. ◣

The New Republican Party

By the late 1970s, three varying groups of conservatives had come to dominate the Republican Party: economic conservatives, foreign policy conservatives, and religious conservatives. All three groups united in 1980 behind Ronald Reagan, a former actor and governor of California. Reagan had an optimistic attitude, a strong strain of patriotism, and a straightforward way of talking that appealed to many people.

Economic conservatives in the party wanted to cut back on government spending, which had grown greatly since the New Deal initiatives introduced by Democratic President Roosevelt in the 1930s. They also wanted to cut down on government regulation of business, which they said hurt American companies and made it difficult for them to grow. That, in turn, limited job growth. Finally, these conservatives argued that the government needed to cut taxes, which would give Americans more money to spend and help stimulate the economy.

Foreign policy conservatives wanted to change American relations with the Soviet Union. They believed that the United States needed to take a tougher stance against Soviet actions and promote anticommunist regimes around the world.

In his 1980 campaign for president, Ronald Reagan told Americans that the nation was mired in an economic crisis and had suffered a loss of prestige abroad—and that he could fix these problems.

Religious conservatives in the party worried about the moral climate of the United States. They looked at rising divorce rates, increases in the number of abortions, and a growing emphasis on sex and violence in movies and television as signs of moral decline. They believed that the government should outlaw abortion and wanted to allow prayer in public schools.

In a televised debate in 1980 with his opponent, Democratic President Jimmy Carter, Reagan explained in simple terms the choice that Americans faced:

THE REPUBLICAN VIEW OF REAGAN

In leading the Republican Party to victory in 1980, Ronald Reagan became one of the most popular figures in the Republican Party's history. Republican leaders who came after him frequently credited Reagan with revitalizing the party and bringing it to dominance. From 1860 to 1980, the Republicans called themselves the Party of Lincoln. After 1980, they changed that name to the Party of Lincoln and Reagan.

Are you better off than you were four years ago? Is it easier for you to go and buy things in the stores than it was four years ago? Is there more or less employment in the country than there was four year ago? Is America as respected throughout the world as it was? ... If you answer all of these questions yes, well then I think your choice is very obvious as to who you'll vote for. If you don't agree ... then I could suggest another choice that you have.

Millions of Americans made the choice Reagan suggested and voted for him. He won the electoral votes of 45 of the 50 states.

Reagan's success was enjoyed by other Republicans as well. Though the Democrats continued to have a majority in the House of Representatives, the Republicans gained 34 seats, their biggest jump in years. In the Senate, Republicans gained 12 seats and became the majority party for the first time since 1955. These gains marked the beginning of a new period during which Republicans came to dominate American politics.

Ronald Reagan appealed to conservative voters who felt the country was in a moral decline.

67

The 1980 election revealed changes in American voting patterns. Nearly recapturing Nixon's success in 1972, Reagan won all of the Southern states except one—Carter's home state of Georgia. In the next six presidential elections, Republicans would win all or most of the states in the South, except when the Democratic candidate came from the South. Reagan also won the votes of a majority of Catholics, becoming only the second Republican, after Nixon in 1972, to do so well among that group. And Reagan won a majority of men who voted—but not a majority of women's votes. Several later elections also showed this gender gap, as journalists called it, in which men tended to support the Republican candidate while women supported the Democrat. When Reagan won re-election in 1984—by an even wider margin—another new voting pattern emerged. He became the first Republican to win the majority of voters under 30.

The Republican Party viewed Reagan's two victories as support from the American people for their calls for change. Taxes were quickly lowered, government regulation of businesses was reduced, and government spending on domestic programs was cut. He also increased military spending and helped governments around the world that were threatened by communism. From 1989 to 1991, Communist governments collapsed in Eastern Europe and the Soviet Union, ending the Cold War. Republicans credit Reagan's policies for those dramatic changes.

Ronald Reagan had once called the Soviet Union an evil empire, but late in his presidency he made historic treaties with Soviet leader Mikhail Gorbachev (right) to reduce the number of nuclear weapons in both the United States and the Soviet Union.

By that time, however, Reagan was no longer in the White House. He had been replaced by George H.W. Bush, who had been his vice president. President Bush helped maintain smooth relations with European countries and with the Soviet Union as Communist governments fell.

In 1990, Iraq's dictator, Saddam Hussein, invaded Kuwait, an oil-rich neighboring country. Bush skillfully engineered a coalition of countries that sent troops to oppose Hussein. When the Iraqi leader refused to leave Kuwait, Bush mounted the Gulf War, in which troops from around the world—led by Americans—quickly and decisively defeated Iraqi troops and liberated Kuwait.

In the wake of the Gulf War victory, Bush enjoyed enormous popular approval. When economic problems developed, however, he could not revive the economy. As a result, he lost his bid for re-election in 1992.

Though Democratic President Bill Clinton held the White House from 1993 to 2001, Republicans made gains during that period. The most dramatic

President George H.W. Bush was unable to turn his foreign-policy successes into a re-election victory in 1992.

came in 1994, when they became the majority party in the House of Representatives for the first time in 40 years.

In 2000, Republican George W. Bush—the son of George H.W. Bush— ran for president against Democrat and former Vice President Al Gore. The result was the closest election in American history. Of the more than 105 million votes cast, only about 540,000 votes

Contract With America

Newt Gingrich (1943–) was the mastermind behind the Republican House victory in 1994. Gingrich was a bold thinker whose ideas helped strengthen the Republican Party. In 1994, Gingrich recruited more than 100 Republican candidates for House seats to endorse a pledge called the Contract with America. This document set out several conservative goals that the candidates promised to enact if Republicans won a majority in the House. When Republicans won that majority, they elected him speaker of the House—the top leadership post in that chamber.

separated Bush and Gore—a difference of less than one half of 1 percent. The difference was equally close in the electoral college, which Bush won by only one vote.

But the election was not settled on election night. Bush's victory came in Florida, where questions arose about the accuracy of the vote counts. Gore asked the state to hold a recount, but soon after the recount began, Bush sued to stop the count, arguing that it was plagued by problems that made it unfair. The case reached the U.S. Supreme Court, which ruled 5 to 4 in favor of Bush. The court's decision awarded Florida's electoral votes to Bush, making him president.

71

George W. Bush became president of a deeply divided nation. Many Democrats believed that the Supreme Court had acted unfairly in ruling as it did. They pointed out that all five of the justices who ruled in Bush's favor had been appointed by Republican presidents.

George W. Bush (right) and Vice President Dick Cheney declared victory after a controversial election in 2000.

Despite the cloud over his presidency, Bush quickly began to move forward on several of the goals he had outlined. He cut taxes, hoping to help the economy advance. He also worked with Democrats to pass a law that dramatically changed public-school education by requiring schools to show that their students were learning in order to continue to receive federal aid.

Then, on September 11, 2001, terrorists mounted a dramatic and deadly attack on the United States. They crashed hijacked commercial airplanes into the two towers of New York City's World Trade Center, as well as the Pentagon—headquarters of the Defense Department—in northern Virginia. A fourth plane, apparently meant to hit a target in Washington, D.C., crashed in a field in Pennsylvania.

The attacks, which killed more than 3,000 people, stunned the country. Nine days later, Bush announced his intention of going after al-Qaida, the terrorist organization that had made the attacks. In a speech to both houses of Congress and televised to all Americans, the president declared a war on terrorism:

> *We will direct every resource at our command—every means of diplomacy, every tool of intelligence, every instrument of law enforcement, every financial influence, and every necessary weapon of war—to the disruption and to the defeat of the global terror network.*

The next month, American troops landed in Afghanistan to destroy al-Qaida training bases there and to overthrow the Taliban, a group that ruled Afghanistan and gave aid to the terrorist group. The troops ousted the Taliban and killed and captured many terrorists, though they could not capture al-Qaida's leader, Osama bin Laden.

President George W. Bush addressed the American people on television shortly after the September 11, 2001, terrorist attacks.

The Bush administration also accused Iraq's dictator, Saddam Hussein, of aiding terrorists and trying to develop weapons of mass destruction. In 2003, the United States and other nations invaded Iraq. The troops quickly overthrew Iraq's government, but creating peace and democracy in that country proved a more difficult task. In addition, no weapons of mass destruction were found.

Though many Democrats and others raised questions about the war in Iraq, Republicans continued to support both that effort and President Bush. But by the November 2004 elections, support had begun to weaken. After the Republicans won the elections, support for the war continued to dwindle until a majority of Americans disapproved of Bush's handling of the presidency. ◣

The Republican Party Today

Chapter

7

The 2004 presidential election was a divisive one, and the news media's coverage of the contest emphasized that division using color codes made popular in the previous election. States that voted primarily Republican were identified by the color red and Democratic-voting states by the color blue. Today the color red has joined the elephant as a visual emblem of the Republican Party.

Today's "red states" are not the same as the Republican strongholds of the party's early days— the geography of the Republican Party has changed greatly over its century-and-a-half history. When the party was founded in the 1850s, it was a party of the Northeast and Great Lakes states, as well as states of the West Coast. Since it was an antislavery party at first, it had little appeal to Southerners.

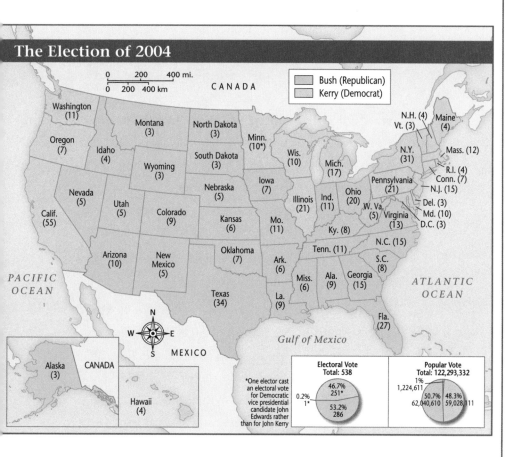

The Election of 2004

| | Bush (Republican) |
| | Kerry (Democrat) |

CANADA

Washington (11)
Montana (3)
North Dakota (3)
Minn. (10*)
N.H. (4)
Vt. (3)
Maine (4)
Oregon (7)
Idaho (4)
Wyoming (3)
South Dakota (3)
Wis. (10)
Mich. (17)
N.Y. (31)
Mass. (12)
Nevada (5)
Utah (5)
Colorado (9)
Nebraska (5)
Iowa (7)
Illinois (21)
Ind. (11)
Ohio (20)
Pennsylvania (21)
R.I. (4)
Conn. (7)
N.J. (15)
Calif. (55)
Kansas (6)
Mo. (11)
W. Va. (5)
Virginia (13)
Del. (3)
Md. (10)
D.C. (3)
Arizona (10)
New Mexico (5)
Oklahoma (7)
Ark. (6)
Ky. (8)
Tenn. (11)
N.C. (15)
S.C. (8)
Texas (34)
La. (9)
Miss. (6)
Ala. (9)
Georgia (15)
Fla. (27)

PACIFIC OCEAN

ATLANTIC OCEAN

Gulf of Mexico

MEXICO

Alaska (3)   CANADA

Hawaii (4)

*One elector cast an electoral vote for Democratic vice presidential candidate John Edwards rather than for John Kerry

Electoral Vote Total: 538
46.7% 251*
0.2% 1*
53.2% 286

Popular Vote Total: 122,293,332
1% 1,224,611
50.7% 48.3%
62,040,610 59,028,111

After the Civil War, it became popular in the South, largely because of the voting strength of recently freed African-Americans. Much of that support ended in 1876, with the end of Reconstruction. For nearly 100 years, the South was solidly Democratic. In the late 1800s, Republicans dominated the Great Plains and the Rocky Mountain states, as areas in those regions became part of the Union.

From the 1930s to the 1970s, states in the original Republican stronghold of the Northeast and Great Lakes regions often voted Democratic. These states had large numbers of manufacturing workers who

The election of 2004 was a close race in which George W. Bush and Dick Cheney were re-elected by a small margin. Republican support in 2004 was strongest in the states colored red.

77

belonged to labor unions. Since the Democratic Party supported unions and the Republican Party favored business owners, these workers often voted for Democratic political candidates. Starting with Reagan's election in 1980, however, many of these states have become up for grabs, sometimes going for one party and sometimes for the other. Meanwhile, the Republicans have developed a solid hold on the South and kept control of the Great Plains and Rocky Mountain states, although they have lost the West Coast.

Geographical shifts can also be seen by looking at the origins of Republican presidents. The first six elected Republican presidents—Abraham Lincoln, Ulysses Grant, Rutherford B. Hayes, James Garfield, Benjamin Harrison, and William McKinley—all came from the Great Lakes states. The most recent four—Richard Nixon, Ronald Reagan, George H.W. Bush, and George W. Bush—all came from the West or South.

Like its geography, some Republican positions have changed over the years. Of course, many of the issues facing the country today are very different from those in the past. Even so, a number of shifts are apparent, most dramatically in the area of race relations. Republicans championed the rights of African-Americans during the Civil War and Reconstruction. They passed constitutional amendments banning slavery, guaranteeing African-Americans equal rights, and giving African-American men the right to vote.

Today, however, many African-Americans think the Republicans ignore the issues that are important to them. That explains why only a tiny percentage of African-Americans belong to the party. In recent years, however, Republicans have made efforts to try to strengthen their appeal to African-Americans.

But the Republicans have maintained many of their original positions. For example, The early Republican Party supported business, which today's Republicans also do. The original Republicans believed strongly in the importance of preserving the Union, and today's Republicans believe in the need for a strong national defense. Moral and religious ideas continue to play an important role in the party. Early Republicans criticized slavery on moral grounds. Today many Republicans oppose abortion or certain kinds of scientific research because they believe them to be immoral.

Who, then, are the people who belong to the Republican Party? Men, Caucasians, Protestants, and people who earn more than $90,000 a year are all more likely to belong to the Republican Party than the rest of the population. Women, African-

PARTY PERCENTAGES

Despite its geographic dominance, the Republican Party is not a majority party. Just under 30 percent of Americans say they are Republicans, slightly less than the approximately 33 percent who call themselves Democrats. Though the percentages are close, the trends favor Republicans. While the percentage of Republicans rose only a little from 1952, the total number of Democrats has fallen dramatically. In 1952, nearly 50 percent of Americans said they were Democrats. The majority of people today— nearly 40 percent—identify themselves as independents.

Americans, Hispanics, Jews, and people who earn less than $30,000 are far less likely than the population as a whole to be Republicans.

What do these modern-day members of the Republican Party believe in? The chart compares Republican and Democratic positions based on statements made in the 2004 party platforms.

REPUBLICAN AND DEMOCRATIC POSITIONS

Issue	Republican Position	Democratic Position
War on terrorism	Fully endorses all actions taken by President Bush, including invasions of Afghanistan and Iraq	Criticizes Bush for invasion of Iraq, which distracted troops from needs in Afghanistan and for alienating possible allies
Patriot Act (law that gives law-enforcement officials new tools to investigate possible terrorists)	Act should be extended as originally written, with full powers to law enforcement	Act should be extended with changes to prevent actions that could endanger the civil rights of Americans
Federal deficit (need to borrow money because the government spends more than it takes in)	Bush economic policies will help the economy grow, thereby cutting the deficit	Bush policies are responsible for the deficit; taxes on wealthiest people and cuts in spending are needed
Taxes	Tax cuts made in first Bush term should be continued to promote economic growth	Tax cuts for the poor and the middle class should be continued, but not for the wealthiest people
Illegal immigrants	Employers who hire illegal immigrants should be punished; illegal immigrants should not be allowed to stay in country	Illegal immigrants with no criminal records who have jobs should be allowed to stay and eventually become citizens
Gun control	Second Amendment ensures the right to own guns; the best way to control guns is to give harsh penalties to those using guns to commit crimes	Second Amendment ensures the right to own guns, but assault weapons should be banned

Issue	Republican Position	Democratic Position
Social Security	System should be changed to allow individuals to control the investment of part of their own contribution	System should not include personal investment
Racial discrimination	Discrimination on the basis of race, gender, or any other factor is wrong; any system that sets aside certain numbers of jobs or places in college for members of certain groups is also wrong	Discrimination on the basis of race, gender, or any other factor is wrong; systems that give advantages to racial or gender groups to redress past discrimination are fair
Abortion rights	Unborn children are protected by the 14th Amendment; opposes abortion and the use of public funds to pay for abortions for poor women	Women's rights to abortion should be protected; public funds should be used to help poor women have the same rights as those with money
Same-sex marriage	A constitutional amendment should define marriage as only involving one man and one woman	This question should be left to individual states
Health insurance	People should be insured through their employers or by buying their own insurance; cutting costs will make insurance more affordable	People should be insured through their employers or by buying their own insurance; the government should cover the health costs of the poor and provide insurance to children without it
Pollution controls	Allowing companies to buy and sell pollution credits is best way to control pollution	Strict pollution controls are needed; any company that causes pollution should pay for cleanup
Energy policy	A combination of increased domestic production, investment in alternative sources of energy, and conservation is needed	The Republican policy is based on oil; there needs to be an emphasis on renewable energy and conservation

Republicans believe that their stands on issues make the party appealing to a majority of Americans. They point to the many election victories they have won in the last few decades as evidence of that appeal. Republicans' success, however, masks trends that could prove challenging to the party. While Republican George W. Bush won both the 2000 and 2004 elections, he did so by very small margins. If he had lost just one key state—Florida in 2000 and Ohio in 2004—he would have lost the election.

If the American people come to believe that a party cannot solve the nation's problems, that party can easily lose its dominance. Such dramatic shifts in power have happened several times over the years, from the fall of the Democrats and the rise of the Republicans in the 1850s to the Democratic triumph of Franklin Roosevelt in 1932 and, more recently, to the rebirth of the Republican Party under Ronald Reagan in 1980.

In the 2006 midterm elections, voters expressed their dissatisfaction with Republican leadership by electing predominantly Democratic candidates to state and federal government offices. Concerns about the budget deficit and the ongoing war in Iraq shifted the balance of power in Washington, giving the Democratic Party control of both the House of Representatives and the Senate. Furthermore, the 2006 vote gave the Democrats control of both legislative chambers in 23 states and improved their position in others.

Still, the Republicans have two great advantages. In recent years, they have controlled the legislatures of many of the states with the most rapidly growing populations. These states will probably receive more seats in the U.S. House of Representatives in the future. Since Republicans control these states' legislatures, they will have the opportunity to draw the lines of congressional districts, and they can do so to give advantages to party members and to hurt the chances of Democrats.

President George W. Bush posed with present and former secretaries of state and defense early in 2006 at the White House. Bush met with the bipartisan group to discuss the war in Iraq.

83

Also, Republicans have a strong central organization. For years, the party has succeeded in raising more money than the Democratic Party, partly because its pro-business policies persuade wealthy business people to donate. The parties use that money to support candidates across the nation and in efforts to identify and persuade potential voters. The gap between money raised by Republicans and that raised by Democrats has been huge. In the 2006 congressional campaign, Democrats narrowed that gap, gaining contributions from business interests that, sensing a possible shift in power, courted the Democrats "just in case." However, Democrats still only raised about 85 percent of the money Republicans did.

Two keys to the party's future will be how its candidates fare among suburban and Hispanic voters. Nearly half of all voters live in suburbs. Since Richard Nixon was elected, the candidate whom suburban voters vote for has generally won the presidential election. Republicans will have to continue to appeal to these voters in order to gain electoral strength.

The other key lies in a growing ethnic group— Hispanics. In early 2000, Hispanics became the largest minority group in the United States. They do not yet form a major voting group, however, since the majority of Hispanics are not registered to vote. The number of people that register has increased

over the years, though, and Hispanic turnout in elections has increased as well. Appealing to these voters can be an important element in winning states where Hispanic voters form a large share of the population, which is true in many states of the South and West.

Republicans have made efforts in recent years to try to win the support of Hispanic and African-American voters.

More than 150 years have passed since a group of antislavery activists gathered to form the Republican Party. In that time, the nation has changed, and the party has as well. For most of its history, this "Grand Old Party" has enjoyed political dominance, taking moral stances and establishing itself as the party of business and national defense. It is hard to believe that it all began in a small Wisconsin schoolhouse. ◣

Timeline

1834

The Whig Party forms to oppose the policies of Andrew Jackson and the Democratic Party.

March 20, 1854

Politicians opposed to the Kansas–Nebraska Act meet in Ripon, Wisconsin, to discuss forming a new antislavery party.

July 6–13, 1854

A state convention of antislavery politicians is held in Jackson, Michigan, taking the name Republican Party.

June 1856

Republicans hold their first national convention in Philadelphia and nominate John Charles Frémont for president.

November 4, 1856

James Buchanan is elected president; Frémont finishes close second; Republicans win 92 seats in the House.

March 6, 1857

The U.S. Supreme Court issues its *Dred Scott* decision, declaring that Congress has no power to ban slavery from territories and that African-Americans cannot be citizens.

August 21–October 15, 1858

Abraham Lincoln and Stephen Douglas stage a series of debates across Illinois in a campaign for a seat in the U.S. Senate.

May 1860

Republicans hold their national convention in Chicago and nominate Abraham Lincoln for president.

1861–1865

Abraham Lincoln serves as the 16th president; the Union and the Confederacy fight the Civil War.

1862

Congress passes the Homestead Act, the Pacific Railroad Act, and the Morrill Land Grant Act, putting in place key Republican programs.

January 1, 1863

Lincoln issues the Emancipation Proclamation, freeing slaves in areas under rebellion.

April 14, 1865

Lincoln is assassinated.

December 6, 1865

The 13th Amendment, abolishing slavery, is ratified.

July 9, 1868

The 14th Amendment, granting citizenship to African–Americans and guaranteeing equal protection of the laws to all Americans, is ratified.

1869–1877

Ulysses S. Grant serves as the 18th president.

1874

Political cartoonist Thomas Nast first uses an elephant to stand for the Republican vote; later it becomes the party's symbol.

February 3, 1870

The 15th Amendment, banning barriers to the right to vote based on race, is ratified.

March 2, 1877

Rutherford B. Hayes is announced as the next president after a disputed election; an arrangement to give the presidency to Hayes includes a promise to remove the last federal troops from the South, ending Reconstruction.

1881

James A. Garfield serves as the 20th president.

1881–1885

Chester A. Arthur serves as the 21st president, taking office after Garfield is assassinated.

1884

Boston Herald first refers to the Republican Party as the GOP.

1889–1893

Benjamin Harrison serves as the 23rd president.

1897–1901

William McKinley serves as the 25th president.

1901–1909

Theodore Roosevelt serves as the 26th president, taking office after McKinley is assassinated; he wins election in 1904.

1909–1913

William Howard Taft serves as the 27th president.

November 1912

Theodore Roosevelt splits from the Republican Party to form the Progressive Party and challenge Taft; Democrat Woodrow Wilson wins the presidency.

April 8, 1913

The 17th Amendment, giving voters power to elect members of the U.S. Senate, is ratified.

Timeline

1921–1923

Warren G. Harding serves as the 29th president.

1923–1929

Calvin Coolidge serves as the 30th president, taking office when Harding dies; he then wins election in 1924.

1929–1933

Herbert Hoover serves as the 31st president.

1929

The Great Depression begins.

1932

Hoover loses to Democrat Franklin Delano Roosevelt, who goes on to win the presidency three more times.

1953–1961

Dwight D. Eisenhower serves as the 34th president.

November 3, 1964

Republican Barry Goldwater loses the presidential election but becomes the first Republican to win electoral votes in the South since Reconstruction.

1974–1977

Gerald R. Ford serves as the 38th president, taking office after Richard Nixon resigns; Ford loses the 1976 election to Jimmy Carter.

November 4, 1980

Ronald Reagan wins the presidency in a landslide victory; Republicans gain a majority in the Senate for the first time since 1955.

1989–1993

George H.W. Bush serves as the 41st president.

November 1994

Republicans win a majority in the House for the first time since 1955.

December 12, 2000

In *Bush v. Gore*, the U.S. Supreme Court orders the recount of Florida votes stopped, giving the disputed 2000 election to George W. Bush.

September 11, 2001

Terrorists attack the World Trade Center and the Pentagon.

October 7, 2001

The United States and its allies begin an invasion of Afghanistan to destroy al-Qaida terrorist training camps and overthrow the Taliban government.

March 20, 2003

The United States and its allies begin an invasion of Iraq to overthrow Saddam Hussein.

On the Web

For more information on this topic, use FactHound.

1 Go to *www.facthound.com*

2 Type in this book ID: 0756524490

3 Click on the *Fetch It* button. FactHound will find the best Web sites for you.

Historic Sites

Lincoln Home National Historic Site
413 S. Eighth St.
Springfield, IL 62701
217/492-4241

Site of Abraham Lincoln's home, which includes material related to his role in the early years of the Republican Party.

Little White Schoolhouse
303 Blackburn St.
Ripon, WI 54971
920/748-6764

The site of the first Republican meeting offers guided tours.

Look for more books in this series

Brown v. Board of Education:
The Case for Integration

The Chinese Revolution:
The Triumph of Communism

The Democratic Party:
America's Oldest Party

The Indian Removal Act:
Forced Relocation

The Progressive Party:
The Success of a Failed Party

The Japanese American Internment:
Civil Liberties Denied

The Scopes Trial:
The Battle Over Teaching Evolution

A complete list of **Snapshots in History** titles is available on our Web site: *www.compasspointbooks.com*

Glossary

abolitionist
person who supported the banning of slavery

amendment
formal change to the U.S. Constitution

annex
claim authority over the land of another nation

bill
proposed law introduced in Congress that must be passed by both the Senate and the House of Representatives and signed by the president or passed again by both houses of Congress to become a law

boss
political leader who holds great power by controlling his party's political organization in a city or a state

conservative
opposed to change, preferring to keep things as they are

impeach
charge an elected official with a serious crime; it can result in removal from office

nativism
movement that reflected preferences for native-born Americans and mistrust of immigrants

patronage
system by which the party in power controls government jobs

platform
statement of political goals made by members of a political party

tariff
tax a government adds to goods imported from another country, which increases the cost of the imports

temperance
reform movement that worked to outlaw the sale and consumption of alcoholic beverages, which were blamed for a host of social problems

territory
area that belongs to the United States but is not yet organized as a state

veto
presidential power to reject a bill passed by Congress; if two-thirds of both houses pass the bill again, they override the veto, and the bill becomes law

Source Notes

Chapter 1

Page 10, line 10: Paul F. Boller Jr. *Presidential Campaigns*. New York: Oxford University Press, 1996, p. 91.

Page 11, line 4: Arthur M. Schlesinger Jr., ed. *History of U.S. Political Parties*. New York: Chelsea House, 1973, p. 1,203.

Page 16, line 8: *Presidential Campaigns*, p. 94.

Chapter 2

Page 21, line 1: James M. McPherson. *The Battle Cry of Freedom*. New York: Ballantine Books, 1989, p. 177.

Page 22, line 3: Roy P. Basler, ed. *The Collected Works of Abraham Lincoln*. New Brunswick, N.J.: Rutgers University Press, 1953, pp. 254–255.

Page 23, line 13: A. James Reichley. *The Life of the Parties: A History of American Political Parties*. New York: Free Press, 1992, p. 123.

Chapter 3

Page 32, line 19: John Woolley and Gerhard Peters. "Democratic Party Platform of 1864." *The American Presidency Project*. 2 Oct. 2006. www.presidency.ucsb.edu/showplatforms.php?platindex=D1864

Page 39, sidebar: "History of the Democratic Donkey." The Democratic National Committee. 2 Oct. 2006. www.democrats.org/a/2005/06/history_of_the.php

Chapter 4

Page 40, line 12: *The Life of the Parties*, p. 153.

Page 42, line 9: Ibid., p. 128.

Page 46, line 12: Foster Rhea Dulles. *America's Rise to World Power, 1898–1954*. New York: Harper & Row, 1954, p. 51.

Source Notes

Chapter 5

Page 52, line 7: John Woolley and Gerhard Peters. "Republican Party Platform of 1924." *The American Presidency Project.* 2 Oct. 2006. www.presidency.ucsb.edu/showplatforms.php?platindex=R1924

Page 54, line 2: U.S. State Department. "Outline of U.S. History." 2 Oct. 2006. http://usinfo.state.gov/products/pubs/histryotln/war.htm

Page 59, line 21: Diane Ravitch, ed. *The American Reader: Words That Moved a Nation.* New York: HarperCollins, 1990, p. 302.

Chapter 6

Page 66, line 19: *Presidential Campaigns,* p. 361.

Page 73, line 25: George W. Bush. "Address to a Joint Session of Congress and the American People." *United States Capitol.* 20 Sept. 2001. 14 Nov. 2006. www.whitehouse.gov/news/releases/2001/09/20010920-8.html

SELECT BIBLIOGRAPHY

Boller, Paul F., Jr. *Presidential Campaigns.* New York: Oxford University Press, 1996.

Bonadio, Felice A., ed. *Political Parties in American History, Vol. 2: 1828–1890.* New York: Putnam's, 1974.

Foner, Eric. *Free Soil, Free Labor, Free Men: The Ideology of the Republican Party Before the Civil War.* New York: Oxford University Press, 1970.

Gienapp, William E. *The Origins of the Republican Party, 1852–1856.* New York: Oxford University Press, 1987.

McGuiness, Colleen, ed. *National Party Conventions, 1831–1988.* Washington, D.C.: Congressional Quarterly, 1991.

McPherson, James. *Battle Cry of Freedom: The Civil War Era.* New York: Ballantine Books, 1989.

Reichley, A. James. *The Life of the Parties: A History of American Political Parties.* New York: Free Press, 1992.

FURTHER READING

Barney, William L. *The Civil War and Reconstruction: A Student Companion.* New York: Oxford University Press, 2001.

Burgan, Michael. *George W. Bush.* Minneapolis: Compass Point Books, 2004.

Haugen, Brenda. *Abraham Lincoln: Great American President.* Minneapolis: Compass Point Books, 2006.

Landau, Elaine. *Friendly Foes: A Look at Political Parties.* Minneapolis: Lerner Publications, 2004.

Strausser, Jeffrey. *Painless American Government.* New York: Barron's, 2003.

Williams, Jean Kinney. *Ronald Wilson Reagan.* Minneapolis: Compass Point Books, 2003.

Index

ABOUT THE AUTHOR

Dale Anderson studied history and literature at Harvard College. He has worked in publishing ever since. He lives with his wife and two sons in Newtown, Pennsylvania, where he writes and edits textbooks and library books. He has written several books for young adults, including books on the Tet Offensive and the Watergate scandal in the Snapshots series.

IMAGE CREDITS

AP/Wide World Photos, **cover**, Corbis pp. **back cover (middle)** and **41**, **2** and **27**, **5** and **60**, **6** and **45**, **9**, **11** and **86**, **36**, **47**, **51**, **53** and **88**, **55**, **56**, **58**, **87** (all) (Bettman), **13** (David J. & Janice L. Frent Collection), **back cover (left)**, **21** and **86** (The Corcoran Gallery of Art), **33** (Museum of the City of New York), **62** (Wally McNamee), **70** (Jean Louis Atlan/Sygma), **back cover (right)** and **72**, **74** and **88**, **83** (Brooks Kraft), **85** (Peter Turnley), **25**, **29**, **65**; Getty Images p. **19**; Library of Congress pp. **15**, **30**, **34**, **38**, **43**, **49**; The Ronald Reagan Presidential Foundation pp. **67**, **69**.